Carousel

Andrea McMahon

BookLeaf Publishing

India | USA | UK

Presentation by *BookLeaf Publishing*

Web: www.bookleafpub.com

E-mail: info@bookleafpub.com

ISBN: 9789360940355

First edition 2024

*To my children, always follow your dreams.
Arriana, Aaurian*

*To my family for always believing in me. John,
Suzanne, Erika, Coby McMahon, Milbern,
Kathryn Goetz*

To my second mom. Maria Sarmiento

*To my favorite school teacher. Marybeth
Skerjanec*

*To my amazing college professor. Stephanie
Weatherill*

*To two of the best coworkers, and friends.
Heather Harris, B.j. Lavender*

*To a wonderful customer with a beautiful soul.
Barb Whitney*

Carousel

A carousel and life:
The thrill of the ride
picking which horse to ride on
like choosing your own destiny.
All of the horses having the same function
but each one different and unique
like the diversity in those that surround you.
Horses rising and falling
like the highs and lows, the joys and sorrows
that have shaped you
Gears grinding, shifting, and moving forward
like when you are changing, learning, and
growing.
Round and around in circles
like the cycles you cannot break.
Music playing
as if to remind you to dance like no one is
watching.
The carousel never stops turning
but like life you make the best of every rotation.

#HelpFindKelsie

I am lost in this world
I wish to come home,
I am not at peace
All my soul does is roam.
My friends and family are
grieving with no answers in sight,
please stop what you're doing
and do what is right.
My family wants peace!
My daughter and I deserve justice.
This case has been botched,
even police were trustless.
My mom is still fighting
she will not give up,
until we are home
she is barely surviving.
She is the best mom,
I would have been too!
But you took my chances
away far to soon.
All because our lives had no value to you.
To much time has gone by,
We need to come Home!
You are the one who deserves to be all alone.
An evil coward you are

with all that you've done.
You took it to far
but we will NOT be forgotten.
You wanted fake dreams.
You do not live in reality.
You have no remorse for our fatality.
Someone do the right thing,
we deserve to be heard.
So please speak up
and just spread the word.
I am lost in this world
I wish to come home,
I am not at peace
All my soul does is roam.

Our Hero

Someday you will lose someone that you can't live without. Your heart will be badly broken, and it wont be your choice, but God has loudly spoken. If I could write a story it would be the greatest ever told, of a kind and loving dad who had a heart of gold. He never looked for praise. He was never one to boast. He went on quietly working for the ones he loved the most. His dreams were seldom spoken. His wants were very few and most of the time his worries went unspoken too. He was always a firm foundation through all our storms of life. A steady hand to hold onto in times of stress and strife. A true friend we could turn to when times were good or bad. One of our greatest blessings, the man that we called Dad. We'll remember all he taught us. We'll hurt but wont be sad. He didn't tell us how to live; he lived; and let us watch him do it. He loved us for who we were and accepted us for who we were striving to become. He held our hands when we were little, helped us grow and show us the way, and he stood by us each and everyday. So many things he did that we cannot repay. The hero of our childhood and latter years as well. Every time we think of him our hearts

are filled with pride. Although we cannot hold
you , we will never let you go, in our hearts
you'll live forever because we love you so.
Please always know we love you and no one can
take your place. The years may come and go but
your memory will never be erased.

Cesar Sarmiento

My eyes filled with tears as I heard the news. It never occurred to me how much I could lose. You were apart of me and I apart of you. When you died a piece of me died too. I'm feeling lost in the world that you left behind. Sometimes I feel like I'm losing my mind. I find myself wishing that it wasn't real. When I think about it pain is all that I feel. Tears fill my eyes and I can barely see, but my heart tells me that he will always be with me. I am glad he feels no pain now, he lives in perfect land. I can still feel the touch of his loving hand. As his smile floods my memories I find myself wishing for just one more year, because I cant picture the rest of my life without you here. Just one more laugh, one more time to see you walk through the door. Another smile, another hug, another day, just one more. You always knew just what to say to anyone having a bad day. I wonder if you knew how many lives you touched. Do you know the people here loved you so much? Do you know how many lives you've changed? How many lives you've completely rearranged? As I look towards the blue sky, I imagine you spreading your wings to fly. Be sure to give your mom a sign so she knows you're in heaven and everything's fine. He is not that far away. His soul lives on, looking down, watching over you and everyone. When you feel sad, and life seems blue, just remember he has his arms wrapped around you. On those special days, times you wish he could see, that cool breeze flowing past you is him saying, "It's me." His love and soul are with you and that is where they stay. As for today remember the best times, the laughter, the song, the good life he lived while he was wrong. Continue his heritage, he's counting on you. Keep smiling and surely the sun will come through. His mind is at ease, his soul is at rest, remembering all how he truly was blessed. Continue traditions, no matter how small. Go on with your life, don't worry about falls. He misses you all dearly so keep up your chin, until the day comes we're together again.

J&L Cafe

My parents bought it when I was four. So I grew up in the restaurant business and that can mean everything. My work ethic, my empathy, even my foul mouth way too young. I've met all kinds of people throughout the years, between coworkers and customers, some of whom I consider family. I can't tell you who means more. It's the young teenager starting out bussing tables and working all the way up to waiting tables. That continue working all the way through their second year at the local community college before they move up and move on. Sending their younger siblings to work to follow the same path. It's the single mom working to support two kids. It's the empty nester with their children all grown. It's the 75 year old widow who isn't ready to retire. She has worked there for nearly as long as my parents have owned it. (Grandma Jude, even to my own children.) It's the cook from the local halfway house that my dad saw potential in. The one who got their life together because someone believed in them, gave them a chance, and a place to grow. My dad would give more than a second chance to the ones he saw that potential in. It's

the customers that have watched me grow up
and I am now watching grow old. I wait on some
couples two or three times a day. Sometimes
questioning if I will have that type of love in
future years. I see pictures of their children/
grandchildren graduating, getting married, and
having kids themselves. Watching them come in
for the first time after they lose a spouse,
(comforting, laughing, crying, and sharing
stories together.) It's the happy hour coffee
drinkers that are there almost daily to have
coffee and share stories and jokes with us and
their friends. It's the community we live in.
Donating to local clubs, schools, and charities is
one of the best ways we give back. The same
community that kept our business open during
COVID when only takeout orders were allowed.
I am grateful for all of these not so random
people that have changed and helped shape my
life. The J&L is so much more than a job to me.
It is my home away from home and it really
does mean everything.

1 in 4

Miscarriage is hard to understand,
why some special babies are taken from this
land.
Her pain will never go away,
because her baby couldn't stay.
A boy or a girl she had no clue.
She'd love no matter what,
that she knew.
She had to say goodbye,
before she got a chance to say hello.
Her body giving birth,
but nothing was to show.
She never got to choose your name,
or play your first peek-a-boo game.
She never saw your twinkling eyes,
or counted the fingers on your hands and the
toes upon your feet.
She never saw your little yawn,
or got to rock you right to sleep.
She never kissed your tiny face,
or saw that little smile.
She never held you in her arms,
but she held you for a while.
She never got to see your face,
or hear your precious laughter.
There is no doubt you would have been
her happily ever after.

50 years

Fifty years ago today you said I do until we're gone. Two hearts joined as one and shared each vow. Because of faith, hope, and love we are celebrating now. Years of wedded bliss that started with a simple kiss. To have and to hold, the love you share is more precious than gold. In sickness and in health, 'til death do you part. Still loving each other with all of your heart. For better or worse; she may not have mentioned one day you may have to carry her purse. It takes the Lord to really build a true love that endures. A love that lasts a lifetime. A special love like yours. A precious band of gold was placed upon two hearts of tender years. The gold was not within the rings nor their faces fair. The gold was there for them to spend when silver coins were rare. It didn't buy them more to have but taught them how to share. They spent it on a loving look. On patience, kindness, and trust. They spent it on the kinds of things that will not wilt or rust. The wonder of this band of gold, if you can comprehend, each time they used their gift of love there was that much more to spend. No doubt it is the sum of all that you are that gathers us here by your side. To celebrate every

year of your love and honor this groom and his
bride. So may you continue to brighten this
world and get just as much as you give.
Enjoying the fruits of the seeds you have sown
everyday for as long as you live.

My mask

I wish to delve into the depths of my mind.
Where sabotage lurks and secrets unwind.
Don't believe my words. They are lies I fabricate
to convince others I'm okay.
The truth is kept farther away.
Don't trust my smile. It is a facade to conceal
undeniable heartache, dreadful shame, and
scarring pain.
Just another link in my life chain.
Don't be convinced by my laughter. It is simply
an echo of my hollow core.
Longing for my senses to restore.
Don't be fooled by my clarity and order. It is
produced in an attempt to control the chaos.
To soothe the storms I come across.
Don't be blinded by the courage I show or the
confidence I wear. It is a shield.
One that I am learning to yield.

I never thought it would be me

A murder with no body.
The victim was my innocence,
stolen with his fists.
Behind closed doors, a silent battle.
A hidden war that no one knew.
It started with slamming doors and holes in the
walls.
Then I was being pushed not only mentally but
physically.
At first he left the marks where no one could
see.
I thought it was my fault.
He put the blame on me.
I tried to change, but the marks he left changed
too.
Soon there was no more hiding the hell that I'd
been through.
He was Dr. Jekyll and Mr. Hyde.
Dr. Jekyll for the world to see.
Mr. Hyde when we were alone
He had no conscience to control him.
To him I was an afterthought,
an object to manipulate,
a service to provide,

a shattered ego to exploit,
someone to deprive.
There never was a funeral because no one knew
I died.
That seems to be what happens when you keep it
all inside.

Finding my voice

- Every 68 seconds an American is sexually
assaulted. Every 9 minutes that victim is a child.
Meanwhile, only 25 out of 1000 perpetrators
will end up in prison. rainn.org -

A life full of hopes, a heart full of dreams.
Sometimes the world is not what it seems.
Wanting to be protected, but that's not how it
goes.
The little secrets that nobody knows.
Searching for safety, but it's not around.
Eager for help, but it can't be found.
Closing your eyes, wishing he'd disappear.
No one should have to go through that fear.
Taking a shower to wash it away,
Only to find out it's here to stay.
Now forever tainted,
From the stroke of a brush that can't be
unpainted.
Going to sleep and wanting to die.
How much more can one person cry?
The bruises and scars, the ones that will never
heal.
The trauma that you can't conceal.
A life of lost hopes and shattered dreams.
Sometimes the world is not what it seems.

Hope

As I journey through my pain,
It's not an easy path to take.
I am on rocky and unknown terrain.
Burying it was my first mistake.
My trauma cuts me open like a knife.
But in my darkness there is hope,
like a great beacon of light.
A chance for me to heal,
to bring myself back to life.
One day everything really will be all right.
Healing will take time.
There will be moments of despair.
I think it's a journey worth the climb.
My healing is possible beyond compare.
My road to recovery will be long,
at the end I will rejoice in song.
My wounds may never disappear,
but my hurt will fade.
A change up in my atmosphere,
the strength to move on is made.
With faith, love, time, and care,
my healed self will be ready to share.

Faith

Along the path less traveled with every winding turn.
In the vastness of the ocean or the darkest of the night.
The guide on my journey, the never ending light.
In the battle of my life with the many trials and tests.
His glory only ever invests.
It remains steadfast and sure,
A spirit so divine and pure.
My faith in God is the foundation where I stand.
Built upon the rock and not on shifting sand.
It's not in grand cathedrals or in the words recited.
A tether that can never be divided.
In every act of kindness,
In small everyday miracles,
In the beauty of the world,
In every tear that's dried.
I find the imprint of God.
A reminder of his presence,
forever by my side.

Ghost

19

Friday the 13th
A spooky, scary ghost hunts
Looking for my grave

Pride

Red neons address
And colors barrage
Intermediate purples notify
Non-spectral blues invite
Bewitched greens attract
Orange sunsets want
Warm yellows insist

My brother

21

Calm, cool, and collected.
Ornery, obnoxious, and original.
Brave, brilliant, and beneficent.
Yankee, yielding, and youngest.

My sister

22

Entertaining, ecstatic, and endearing.
Radiant, rambunctious, and rare.
Impactful, insightful, and intelligent.
Keen, kindred, and karaoke.
Amazing, ambitious, and adorable.

Stoney Bologna

23

Anytime is good
A natural, pungent smell
Yes the perfect toke

Timing or Coincidence

When my gut feeling was right all along.
Timing? Coincidence?
When people believe in me, igniting and
growing my passion for writing.
Timing? Coincidence?
When I meet a stranger that changes my life and
becomes a best friend.
Timing? Coincidence?
When I was in a rollover accident and the seat
belt I happened to be wearing saved my life.
Timing? Coincidence?
When I hit the brakes at exactly the right
moment to avoid a collision.
Timing? Coincidence?
When my children came into my life saving me
and making everything so much better.
Timing? Coincidence?
When I write and share a poem that can even
bring a stranger to tears.
Timing? Coincidence?
When I realize some of my best writing comes
from a raw and vulnerable place. About the
people or events that have made the biggest
impact on my life.
Timing? Coincidence?
Sometimes a coincidence can happen at the
perfect timing.